The Private Diary of
Scarlett O'Hara

by
Cathy Crimmins
and
Tom Maeder

DOVE
B O O K S

ISBN 0-7871-0728-X

Printed in the United States of America

Dove Books
8955 Beverly Boulevard
West Hollywood, CA 90048

Distributed by Penguin USA

Text design and layout by Carolyn Wendt
Jacket illustration, design, and layout by Rick Penn-Kraus

First Printing: July 1996

10 9 8 7 6 5 4 3 2 1

CONTENTS

ACKNOWLEDGMENTS

We would like to thank the following people, who aided us in our extensive research: David O. Selznick, Clark Gable, Jimmy Carter, Al Jolson, Br'er Rabbit, Margaret Mitchell, Thomas Mitchell, Flannery O'Connor, Kelly, Sara, Morgan, and Max O'Hara, Virgil Tibbs, William Faulkner, Chang and Eng Bunker, Harriet Tubman, Leslie Howard, Boo Radley, Truman Capote, Gomer Pyle, Johnny Cash, Carson McCullers, Vivien and Harper Leigh (Lee), Pat Conroy, Curtains Unlimited, Jed Clampitt, Ted Turner, Newt Gingrich, Hattie McDaniel, Atticus Finch, Joellen Brown, Thomas Wolfe, Mr. Peanut, Elvis Presley, the Deliverance Banjo Albino, Olivia de Havilland, Dr. Quinn, Medicine Woman, Dolly Parton, Louis Pasteur, Lestat, the Steel Magnolia Society, Robert E. Lee, Barney Fife, Lew and George Wallace, Huey Long, Conway Twitty, Uncle Tom, Davy Crockett, Paul Bocuse, Jesse Helms, Tennessee Williams, Jefferson Davis, Frederick Douglass, Little Richard, Ann Carson, Norma Rae, Willie Nelson, Mason and Dixon, Colonel Sanders, Jesse Helms, Gennifer Flowers, Hrotsvitha of Gandersheim, Louis Armstrong, Fannie Flagg, and Bill and Hillary Clinton.

FOREWORD

In April 1989, We Dig the South, Inc., a contract archeological research organization based in Venice, California, was hired by Clayton County, Georgia, to undertake a study near the future site of a fast-food restaurant. Federal regulations require that no public work may commence without first ascertaining whether historically or culturally significant artifacts will be destroyed in the process. At the time, there was little reason to believe that the planned work—laying a new sewer line to the "Tara" Taco Bell franchise—could harm anything at all, but government requirements must be met.

From May 1989 to September 1993, senior archeologists Cathy Crimmins and Tom Maeder supervised excavation of the site. The only artifacts discovered were four bottle caps, six partially burnt matches, one Camel cigarette butt, and a 1984 penny. Then, late in the afternoon of September 19, 1993, a graduate student working forty-nine feet below ground level gave a surprised yelp of delight. Her shovel had hit a solid mass, which proved to be a wooden chest of the sort used to transport clothing before the era of the steamer trunk.

The wood of the chest had largely decayed, leaving only the brass hinges, clasps, and an oval plate with the ornate initials "S.O.B." The contents, too, had mostly succumbed to the ravages of time, but a few items were miraculously preserved, including two horse pistols, one house key, one Abraham Lincoln Halloween mask, one pair of manacles, one buggy whip, one woman's corset, one man's corset, and several unmentionables.*

Most exciting of all were eight leather-bound diaries and twenty-six loose sheets of paper, all protected in a separate tin box. The covers of the diaries had disintegrated, and the paper was in exceptionally poor condition. Extensive conservation treatment, however, made it possible to preserve the paper and visually enhance the writing on this collection of documents. Something of inestimable value had been discovered—"S.O.B." referred to none other than Scarlett O'Hara Butler. Crimmins and Maeder had discovered the secret diaries of the woman behind the novel *Gone With the Wind.*

These documents reveal that the real Scarlett O'Hara was quite different from the person previously depicted on page and screen. Margaret Mitchell, whose ancestors had made a hobby of spying on the O'Hara family, driving them nearly mad with incessant snooping, grossly misrepresented many aspects of Ms. O'Hara's life. One can, indeed, surmise that Scarlett O'Hara buried this trunk expressly to keep her deepest secrets safe from the Mitchells' prying eyes.

This startling account of Scarlett O'Hara's private life is, unfortunately, marred by several long and inexplicable gaps, some of one or two years duration, one of them more than seven years long. We may never know whether O'Hara simply neglected to keep up her diary

---

*The unmentionables are on permanent loan to the Sex Museum of Stockholm, Sweden, where scholars are preparing a monograph entitled "Sex Toys of the Antebellum South."

during these periods, or whether entries were subsequently lost or destroyed. The presence of the twenty-six loose pages, all evidently once part of bound volumes, suggests that the O'Hara diaries suffered some damage even during their author's lifetime. One can only hope that the ongoing excavations at the Taco Bell site will unearth additional materials.

Truth, people say, is stranger than fiction. Here, for the first time, is the truth. The following pages contain many surprising revelations about the complex character of Scarlett O'Hara, a tormented woman seeking her identity in the Old South, who at times embraced the joys of learning and discovery, and at others reveled in the simple role of air-headed sexpot.

A scholarly edition of Ms. O'Hara's diary is in preparation but will not be completed until 2010. In the meantime, we present these unadorned documents to satisfy the general public's curiosity about a major figure in American culture.

PART I

Belles Are Clinging

The Early Tara Years

Though only sixteen at the time this diary begins, Scarlett was physically and intellectually precocious, but often confused by the world around her. In these entries, she grapples with issues of sexual identity and the role of southern females during the halcyon days before the Civil War.

March 13, 1861

$\mathscr{D}$ear Diary,

I've been saying "Tomorrow is another day" a lot recently, but then I got to thinking: Is it? Get up, mope and whine, think about men, think nasty thoughts about other women, preen, have Mammy cinch my little waist, stuff myself with pancakes and ham, feel ill half the day, flirt a bit, dote on Daddy, idolize Mommy, make assorted catty remarks, get undressed, go to bed. No, I think tomorrow is the same day as today, over and over and over again.

March 15, 1861

$\mathscr{D}$ear Diary,

That Mitchell family. Such poor white trash with such uppity aspirations! They sit around evenings when good folk ought to be doing their mending and needlework, scribbling away at sheets of paper, saying that one day, you'll see, they'll write the great American novel, whatever that is. I see them everywhere I go. One of them was even asking me how big my waist is. I don't think they're writing any novel at all. They're just writing nasty, false things about the rest of us, thinking they'll have the last word because most everybody else here is illiterate.

P.S. Not that I don't think I'd be a great subject for a book. If someone ever writes my biography I'd like to be portrayed as a catty little small-waisted, big-breasted, magnolia-skinned, green-eyed bitch without a brain. Smart girls get nowhere, especially here in the South.

March 18, 1861

$\mathcal{D}$ear Diary,

Today Daddy and I were enjoying one of those touching southern moments, strolling up the path in the gloaming, with all the land, the land—the only thing that lasts—strewn about everywhere, and the soil and the birds and the bugs and the mint juleps clinking over the hilltops, and Daddy staggering up the path dead drunk . . . well, you get the picture. Then we saw Momma with her bonnet and shawl in the dim shadows by the porch with Mammy following close behind, looking fierce, carrying a leather satchel and wheeling an IV pole.

"Missus O'Hara gwine do brain suhjury on dem dere darn po' wi'te trash Slatterys," Mammy said. "An' he'ah da suppah's gettin' col' . . ."

"Yes, yes, Mammy," Daddy broke in impatiently. "Where are you going, Ellen?"

"Mrs. Slattery has a subdural hematoma, Gerald. All the doctors think she's doomed, but I have a theory that it's the intracranial pressure that causes the damage. If I operate quickly enough I should be able to stabilize her. If I enter through the . . ."

"Oh, those Slatterys! If they can't pay for a doctor to treat them they should just suffer the consequences!"

"Now, Gerald, you know I believe we should have universal health coverage. I've been thinking of writing to my cousin over in Arkansas to see whether she doesn't want to start some sort of initiative. . . ."

March 21, 1861

*D*ear Diary,

Ashley Wilkes, that brainy hunk, stopped by the plantation today raving about some book he just bought, Bartlett's *Familiar Quotations.* It was kind of interesting. Some folks, it seems, are remembered just for things they said. "The redcoats are coming!" Must have been a fashion designer. "Give me liberty or give me death!" Strikes me as pretty silly, though it's a good line. *I* plan to get famous for *doing* things, not talking about them, but maybe I shouldn't take any chances. So I'm trying to come up with a catchy slogan for myself. Then I'll say it all the time, and one day people will remember me for it, and I'll get in Mr. Bartlett's book too. I thought of "Hot-cha-cha-cha!" but that doesn't sound dainty, like something a raven-haired beauty with a seventeen-inch waist would say. "Twenty-three skidoo!" doesn't make any sense. "Damn the torpedoes, full speed ahead!" has a fine ring, but may not be suited to casual situations like going to balls and knocking around the plantation. "Tara-ra-boom-de-yay!" includes the name of Daddy's house, but seems a little stupid. I'm favoring "Fiddle-dee-dee" at the moment, though it might be a little too namby-pamby.

March 27, 1861

$\mathscr{D}$ear Diary,

Mother and I had a touching mother-daughter talk today, to prepare me for the day when she tragically dies of some infectious disease and I am left to fend for my little self in the world. "Scarlett, honey," she said, "I have some good news and some bad news. You are half French, half Irish, all southern, and all woman. That, dear, is the worst possible combination anyone could imagine. It means that by nature you are stubborn, self-centered, greedy, prone to drinking and violent outbursts, irrational, manipulative, supremely arrogant, and absolutely determined to have your own way no matter what you wreck in the process." I asked what the bad news was. "Actually, that was it," she replied. I thought she was joking, but she wasn't. I sometimes think I will never understand mother. "Well, fiddle-dee-dee," I said, trying out my new motto. Mother doesn't seem to like it. She's so serious. "But the good news," she said, "is that you're really cute and have an inexplicable charm, so even though at heart you're such a rotten little bitch—and, my darling, I mean that in the nicest possible way—you do stand a chance in life. You can probably marry as many husbands as you want. Just try to do them one after the other, rather than at the same time."

April 2, 1861

𝒟ear Diary,

Something's funny about Mammy. I was asking Suellen and Careen—did you ever notice that when she hugs you, her breasts feel kind of like they're stuffed with balls of cotton? They claimed not to notice. And one day, when it was really hot, I could swear I saw some of the color rubbing off of Mammy's face. I intend to get to the bottom of this.

April 3, 1861

𝒟ear Diary,

Today I barged in on Mammy in the outhouse, and she was piddling standing up! I said, "Are you really a man, Mammy? After all, you always wear those strange men's shoes."

She began laughing and snorting, and her nose hairs bristled in the early morning light.

"Why, honey chile, you gwine done say the goshdarn foolishest thangs! This here is my A-fri-kann voodoo way of relievin' myself. My grandmammy done taught me it so's thats you can pee and run 'way from the white folk at the same time. Listen up, girlfriend, I is one hunnert percent woman!"

April 5, 1861

*D*ear Diary,

Snuck into Mammy's room today and found a complete makeup kit, the kind for the theater. Lots of "foundation" with brown color. Maybe she has a bad complexion, but I think she's hiding something.

April 6, 1861

*D*ear Diary,

I asked Mammy today why she never had any children of her own, and she mumbled something about not having the right equipment for it. Come to think of it, I've never seen any men around Mammy. What's the story?

P. S. I could swear I saw a blond hair creeping out from under her turban today.

April 8, 1861

*D*ear Diary,

The most shocking thing! My mommy and mammy *kissing* in the hallway upstairs. What gives?

April 9, 1861

𝒟ear Diary,

Okay, so here it goes. I had a terrible nightmare, and I needed my mommy. I went to her room, and instead of Pa, there was a strange, very handsome thin blond man next to her. When I arrived they were kissing and hugging and groaning and humping up and down.

"Who the hell are you?" I screamed at the man.

"Why, Miss Scarlett, don' ya wanna come and kiss your ol' mammy?" said the man.

Then I noticed this enormous dress standing, padded, by itself in the corner, plus a pair of ugly men's shoes and a turban.

"Katie Scarlett," said my mother, "I know this is difficult, but Mammy—I mean Phillipe—and I are special friends. He is the love of my life."

Well, I was just dumbfounded. I ran out of the room immediately, right as ol' Mammy/Phillipe lit up a smelly cigar, and I ran smack dab into Daddy in the hallway.

"Oh, so you know now?" asked Pa, searching my face for clues to my reaction.

"Fiddle-dee-dee, Daddy—life is so confusing," I said, running to my room and locking the door.

April 10, 1861

*D*ear Diary,

All right. I cried throughout the night. I've had a whole day to think, and I'm starting to calm down. But this discovery has shaken my beliefs entirely. I mean, are all the other mammies on plantations around here really just ex-boyfriends, or is my family simply weird? Daddy knocked at my door, and he tried to explain. Told me my mommy's true love never did die the way most people thought, and that he showed up a couple of weeks after my parents were married. Daddy knew he'd lose Mom if he didn't give in to the idea of having Phillipe around the place. But, naturally, they couldn't have her old beau living with them as himself, and Phillipe had always had a flamboyant side, so they hit upon him doing this black mammy impersonation thing. Phillipe calls himself a method actor, whatever that is, and he took the role very seriously, apprenticing himself to other local mammies and reading up on African folktales and songs. I must say, he's been very convincing, and he doesn't seem to want to stop—says that life is a drag, but he must go on. Guess a part of me will always think of him as Mammy, and I think he wants it that way. I promised him that I would never reveal his identity, and that it would never be a problem, since everyone else around here is too stupid to catch on. Only thing is, am I *really* literally Mammy's daughter? I haven't gotten up the nerve to speak to Pa about the whole paternity issue.

April 12, 1861

$\mathscr{D}$ear Diary,

I've always appreciated Mammy's straightforward attitude toward life, and now that I know she's really a man, it explains a lot of things. Like that last barbecue over at Twin Oaks, when she insisted that I eat before I go over there. You see, Mammy has definite ideas about what a lady shouldn't do in public, and she makes me get all sorts of things out of the way before I go to a party. Like she makes me eat beforehand just so I'll seem dainty. And then she makes me drink myself into a stupor and pass out just so's I won't do it at the party. And then she brings in a couple of cute beaux and makes me have sex with them in all sorts of positions so I won't do anything like that when I'm over at the neighbors'. With practical thinking like that, it stands to reason that she's a man.

April 24, 1861

$\mathscr{D}$ear Diary,

Today was awful. Fortunately, as I always say, you can bet your bottom Confederate dollar that the sun will come out tomorrow, which is another day. This afternoon we had some people over to Tara. They were all babbling mindlessly about sports and impending war and whatnot. Finally the girls retired upstairs to unlace their stays and be fanned by pickaninnies with peacock feathers, so I snuck down to the library for some intellectual stimulation. Read a bit of Darwin's latest opus, *On the Origin of Species.* It is well written and provocative, but

I don't accept his slow-motion notion of species evolving. Personally, I favor the Lamarckian view, in which experience produces physical change that is handed down from one generation to the next. How else can we explain the difference between Confederates and Yankees, genetically so similar, yet such worlds apart? I should write to Mr. Darwin and tell him that if he wants to study evolution in action, he should forget about the Galapagos Islands and just come to Georgia. Why look at finches when the Tarletons are at his disposal?

April 27, 1861

$\mathscr{D}$ear Diary,

Okay—this has got to stop! For the third time this month I found the darkies outside throwin' balls through my hoop skirts. They claim it's a new game. "Basketball" they call it, but I don't care—I don't want my underwear being used by darkies, no matter how talented they are.

"Look at me dunk," yelled one of them called Magic, a handsome, strapping young thing, as he plunked the ball through the metal form of my skirt hoops. (I have to admit, Diary, that he is mighty cute!)

"Shootin' hoops," that's what some of the others call it. And I will shoot *them* if I catch them messin' with my underthings one more time.

May 1, 1861

$\mathscr{D}$ear Diary,

Today an important cotton-cloth manufacturer from Manchester, England, came to visit Daddy to discuss buying our cotton. I never realized how funny those English people talk. Freddy Engels brought along his friend Karl Marx. They have very strange ideas, I must say. Kept talking about opium for the people in churches, and even though they seem to think everyone should be equal (even slaves!), they are *the* most class conscious people I ever met, always talking about international social lists and the like. Mr. Marx sneered at us something awful. Even though his manners are disgusting, he put on airs like we weren't good enough for his company, probably because we don't own as much land or as many slaves as he does. The Tarletons stopped by and Marx and Engels tried to discuss economic history with them, which was a hoot, but I guess they did about as well as Marx and Engels did at coon hunting later in the day.

May 18, 1861

$\mathscr{D}$ear Diary,

A mathematician came by for juleps today and said he wanted to teach me computations, but I think he was really after something else. "A seventeen-inch waist?" he said. "Well, let's see. . . . The circumference equals pi times the diameter, so 17 divided by 3.14 equals 5.41 inches. Now let me just measure how wide you are there to confirm this calculation."

Well, I let him do that, and it came out pretty nearly correct, though he did have to measure several times, front to back and side to side, and then he measured a few times higher up and quite a lot of times down below to make sure that his measuring technique was, as he said, all that it should be. Then he said he was going to teach me how to compute volumes. Two hemispheres, he said, make one sphere, and the volume of a sphere is $\frac{4}{3}\pi r^3$. So, he said, he just needed to measure, quite accurately, the radius of one of my hemispheres, and. . . . Well, at that point I had had enough. It seemed to me he was just using mathematics as a pretense. So I led him upstairs and went over some *real* figures with him. He said afterward that he really was interested in mathematics, and I said that was nice, but that he had all the time in the world for that—tomorrow is another day—while the night is made for love. So I did him again. "That's two. I'm teaching you arithmetic." And again. "That's three."

June 1, 1861

$\mathscr{D}$ear Diary,

A Mr. Turner and his wife, Barbarella, passed through on the way to the Barney Fife plantation. He said he's in the business of colorizing photographs. Mammy told him that she was already colorized, thank you very much, and that she had spent much of her life keeping white girls like me out of the sun so that we wouldn't get colorized. He left looking puzzled, saying maybe he'd come back in a hundred years or so and try again.

June 26, 1861

*D*ear Diary,

I wonder why, whenever I open the door of our house or drive up to the front porch in a buggy, this music swells up and drowns out everything else, even the birds singing. "Wooo WOOOOO woo woo," it goes. Did you ever hear of any other houses that come with their own music?

June 28, 1861

*D*ear Diary,

The musical mystery has been solved. Today I saw Pa come out from behind the bushes leading a children's darky choir. Seems he trains them to sing on cue whenever he wants anyone to be impressed with how grand Tara is.

"Saves me a lot of money," he said. "Tara might get a little shabby at times, but music is a real mood enhancer, and it makes people feel they're seeing the Taj Mahal. It's a nice tune, eh, Scarlett? Wooo WOOOOO woo woo. . . . A soundtrack is very important to a house."

"Soundtrack?" I said.

"Aye. It's a little idea I have. You see, someday I believe that everything people do will be accompanied by music. I only wish I didn't have to use these children's choirs—their voices change real quick, and then I have to train 'em all over again."

July 4, 1861

$\mathscr{D}$ear Diary,

Today was such a confusing day, I can't bear to think of it. I hope tomorrow will be another one. That darn party began to get on my nerves, what with the men either snuffling around me with puppy-dog looks on their faces or else strutting about talking war, and the girls babbling about the boys or throwing me catty looks. What dullards. I wish I could chuck this life and do something interesting with myself, like maybe go into the lumber business. I kept ducking into Twelve Oaks for a nip at the Wilkes' whiskey and then a quick gargle with cologne, but everywhere I went there was some decorative southern gentleman lolling about in his spiffy clothes and shiny boots, saying Oh, Miss Scarlett this or Miss Scarlett that.

By midafternoon I was pretty well plastered and ready for some fun. But the men were out getting creamed in a masters-versus-slaves basketball game—how it has caught on!—and the women were all upstairs getting unlaced and taking their naps. Then I saw Melanie. She was sneaking downstairs with her clothes half undone to get herself a bite to eat. I never realized before how attractive she is, in an odd sort of way. Her slim boyish figure somehow thrilled me. I followed her along the hall, watching the gentle swinging of her shoulders and slim hips, and got really turned on. "Melanie!" I called, and motioned her into the library. "What is it, Scarlett, honey?" she said, demurely gathering her bodice up over her flat chest. "Do you have a secret to tell me?" I looked into her quiet brown eyes and blurted out, "I love you, Melanie! I want you! Let's get it on right here and now on the library floor!" Melanie looked surprised. She fluttered her eyelids and raised one placid hand in its black lace glove to her lips, gave a little gasp and said, "Why, Scarlett, this is such a surprise. I admire you more than anyone in the world, and I could probably come to love you, too. But I am going to marry Ashley!" "So what?" I said. "I'm going to marry Ashley too, one day, probably, among all the other husbands I expect to have. But why should that get in our way? We're rich white people in the South—we can do whatever we please!"

Well, Diary, Melanie would have none of it. I pleaded and I shouted and I smacked her silly, but she just kept simpering, "It cannot be, Scarlett. I'm going to marry Ashley." She rejected me—me, Scarlett O'Hara. No man, woman _____* has ever resisted my advances before. I was furious. After that little twit slipped out of the room I picked up a brass spittoon and threw it across the room, shattering the marble mantelpiece over the sofa. "This will never do!" said a deep voice from the depths of the sofa. "What's going on, Rhett? Are the Yankees attacking?" said another deep voice. Suddenly the heads and bare shoulders of that Rhett Butler man and Ashley Wilkes popped up over the back of the couch, their hair all messed. "Why, howdy, Scarlett!" said Ashley. "Would you like to join us?" "Yes, do!" said Mr. Butler, with a wicked look on his face. I was dreadfully insulted by their suggestion. We O'Haras never share.

---

*A word written here was carefully obliterated in the diary. Image enhancement at the Jet Propulsion Laboratory in Pasadena reveals that Ms. O'Hara had originally written "or animal."

July 17, 1861

𝒟ear Diary,

Met the most boring slave today named Uncle Remus. He keeps telling endless stories, and he brought a rabbit to eat for dinner that tasted a lot like tar. Zippety doo-dah, my foot.

PART II

Binge and Siege

Wartime Atlanta

When Scarlett realized that Ashley Wilkes was going to marry Melanie, or possibly Rhett, she flew into a snit and married wimpy Charles Hamilton. The marriage was brief. Charles had just enough time to impregnate Scarlett before dying of measles. Scarlett moved in with Charles's Atlanta relative, the loopy Aunt Pittypat.

June 23, 1862

𝒟ear Diary,

Had a baby boy last week—a present from that nincompoop Charles. Hope the little carpet-rat will get some of my brains. I just came out of the laudanum yesterday, and Mammy tells me the infant's name is "Wade." She says I insisted on it, but I think I might have been asking how much I "weighed" afterward, since I'm determined to get back to my usual ninety-four pounds.

July 30, 1862

𝒟ear Diary,

Being a war widow is such a drag. I have to associate with all sorts of boring ladies working for good causes. Today I met Robert E. Lee's halfwitted sister, Sara, and I was already sick to death of hearing about her. "Nobody doesn't like Sara Lee!" says Aunt Pittypat over and over again. This lady makes the strangest cakes, which she peddles door to door to make money for the troops. The icing on top of them is very thick and all in one piece. If I didn't know better I'd swear she freezes them somehow—maybe she leaves them in the icehouse. Anyway, they taste like cardboard, so they keep forever.

Mrs. Meade told me that once someone opened the door and surprised Sara Lee by throwing a pie in her face. She still didn't get the message. Hope her brother is smarter.

August 6, 1862

*D*ear Diary,

Oh, how I hate this mourning business. Everyone insists that I have to wear black all the time, can't dance, can't sing, can't flirt, can't do anything. All because Charles, my husband, that pill, has been dead for less than a year. That's a lot longer than we were married, isn't it? But I'm supposed to stay in mourning for five years or something, like some old widow woman. Yuch! And there's supposed to be a wonderful party tomorrow, some fair and ball to raise money for that awful old Confederate Cause! I *hate* the war. All it does is take the men away and drive up the price of luxury items.

August 25, 1862

*D*ear Diary,

I got to go to the ball anyway, because the McLure girls are away and the Bonnell girls have the measles, and somebody needed to tend that booth, selling knickknacks for the Cause. Then I was itching to dance, but Aunt Pittypat wouldn't let me until that horrible Captain Butler bid a lot of money for the honor of the first reel with me. People were aghast, but it seemed all right if I did it for the Cause, especially since he was paying in gold.

August 26, 1862

$\mathcal{D}$ear Diary,

Went for a carriage ride with that horrible Captain Butler today. Aunt Pittypat didn't like it, but Captain Butler said he would give another hundred dollars in gold to the Cause, so she had to say it was all right.

August 27, 1862

$\mathcal{D}$ear Diary,

Went for a walk with some handsome young soldier. I don't know his name. Actually, "walk" is probably not the right word, as Dr. Meade amputated one of his legs yesterday and he hasn't been fitted for an artificial limb yet. Aunt Pittypat thought it was unseemly, but I told her it was all for the Cause. Just think of that poor boy, so far from home, with no loved ones to listen to his fears or show him that somebody cared whether he lived or died. And if worst came to worst, he would probably donate a dollar or two. I never believed much in the Cause before, but I am beginning to realize that it has its redeeming features.

August 28, 1862

𝒟ear Diary,

Went to a party with three soldiers. Had a wonderful time, staggering home around 2 A.M. Aunt Pittypat was waiting in the parlor, absolutely irate, saying, "How could you do that, with poor Charles dead hardly a year?" I said, "Charles who?" I honestly wasn't trying to provoke her, I just kind of forgot. Well, she said I *would* not go out again, and that I would just stay inside for years and years or else be sent home to Tara until a respectable amount of time had passed, which probably means until I am a shriveled old hag of thirty-five and the only man who will look at me with any interest is an undertaker. But I said, "Aunt Jiffy-pop"—I'm afraid I was a bit tipsy and forgot her name for a moment—"Aunt Jiffypop, I didn't really *want* to stay out so late with those men, but they were our boys in butternut and gray, our noble soldiers fighting the nasty Yankees for God and the Confederacy, and I felt it was my duty. They're so lonely, Aunt Clippityclop, and they need someone to keep them company, someone to talk to them, to smile at them, to sit on their laps, to keep them from drinking alone. It's all for the Cause!"

August 29, 1862

𝒟ear Diary,

Went skinny-dipping with another couple of soldiers today, then passed the afternoon drinking moonshine. They gave me two rings, a bracelet, and a lovely gold necklace. Aunt Triptrap, predictably, was upset. "Swimming naked with a bunch of strange men?" she asked. I said they weren't strange, they were just Confederates I hadn't known before. As for being naked, I pointed out that I didn't own a black bathing suit, and it would have been unseemly for me to wear any other color while I was still in mourning for Charles, so I had done the best I could. Melanie said she thought I was being very sensitive, the silly little dolt, and that I had certainly tried my hardest. Aunt Flapjack then went on about that jewelry, and how decent girls shouldn't accept anything but candy or flowers or a book of poems or a small bottle of Florida water, but never anything expensive or anything to wear. I said the jewelry was stuff I was going to sell off to raise money for the Cause, but that, following that horrid Captain Butler's example, I figured I should hold onto it for a few days or months or years, until the price went up and I could do even more for our brave boys so far away.

August 30, 1862

𝒟ear Diary,

Aunt Flippetyflop caught me doing two soldiers on the parlor couch. "And with poor Charles dead hardly a year," she moaned, taking a whiff of her smelling salts. "Lady, Charles was not too lively in bed even before he died." It's probably a good thing she didn't know about the other six guys who had just left. Anyway, after my roused rebels buttoned up and toddled off I told her I was only doing what I thought best—that otherwise they would be dreadfully horny, and perhaps would be reduced to autoeroticism, which drives them insane and gives them hairy palms and generally goes against all the South stands for. "Well," she said, and I could see she was wavering. So I told her that the guys had paid me too, and that I was donating part of my earnings to the Cause, and of course then she gave in completely and said I was the most saintly girl on earth to do so much for the Confederacy, and how proud Charles would be to know of his wife's devotion.

September 12, 1862

*O*h, Diary!

Did I hit on something or what? Half the widows this side of forty, most of the women whose husbands are off getting shot up by Yankees, and an awful lot of cute unmarried young things who want to experiment a bit before settling down are now working for me. And here they all said I had no head for practical things. I've already nearly run old Belle Watling out of business. My place is right in the heart of Atlanta, with a big sign over the front door that says SCARLETT'S PLEASURE DOME (FOR THE CAUSE). It's perfect. Our brave boys have a blast, our brave girls have the time of their lives, we women are earning enough money to buy nice things for ourselves even at those profiteers' prices, and of course we give one percent of the take to the Cause. Aunt Hoochy-Coochy sits in the front hall as a chaperone to make sure nothing improper happens. I have accordingly laid down strict rules that only proper behavior is permitted in the front hall, but that everywhere else, anything goes! After only one week in business, my net averages $140,000 per day, and rising.

September 18, 1862

$\mathscr{D}$ear Diary,

That young Carver kitchen slave sure is smart. He's been experimenting with peanuts, trying to think of things to make from them, and now he's come up with something he calls a "synthetic fiber," which he named "Pea-on." Says it will replace cotton, and nobody, black or white, will ever have to wear his fingers to the bone picking the stuff again. Better living through chemistry, he says his motto is. I don't know. It sounds like a good idea, but when I mentioned it to Aunt Hippety-Hop she said she would be consarned if she was going to dress in peanuts. I told her, no, George didn't want her to dress in peanuts, they would take the peanuts and crush 'em up and do something with them first. But she simply didn't understand. She said she didn't care, she wasn't going around with any peanuts on her that had been crushed and done something with. At that point Rhett interrupted the conversation, as he always does, latching onto some little bit out of context that he hasn't understood in the first place, and he said he never knew Aunt Hippety-Hop *had* a penis at all, crushed or otherwise, but that he found this quite interesting. And she asked what *was* he talking about, and they got into a conversation so strange that I finally had to leave the room, because I figured eventually they would realize what each other was talking about and then all hell would break loose.

September 28, 1862

𝒟ear Diary,

Today Mammy came upon me in the outhouse, retching.

"Miss Scarlett," she said, "what is ailing you?"

"Nothin.' I'm just keeping my figure," I assured him.

"Oh, thas jus what your mother done, too," said my poor old Mammy, dabbing at her/his eyes. "I wondered if she had passed it along to you."

It was a poignant moment as I wiped off the vomit from my top lip and Mammy and I stood in silence remembering what a dietary pioneer my mother had been. You see, Diary, Mother had something of a medical bent, and she was obsessed with discovering the secret of how a woman could keep her figure. For a while she tried surgically removing a rib or two from obese young black women to make their waists smaller, but that only worked for so long, because the darkies would start downing those hush puppies, and before you knew it, fried foods would make them balloon up just like your average mammy. Then Mother began a series of dietary experiments. After trying about twenty different diets, she hit upon the perfect combination of bingeing and purging to keep a woman svelte forever.

The plan was simple: Eat grits for breakfast and lunch, then eat a reasonable meal for dinner and vomit it up. She tested it on our young slave girl Bulimia, who lost twenty-six pounds in only two weeks! It's a shame Mother died before she could market her idea. She was planning to call it Ultra-Grit-Fast, and she had lots of celebrities, even Robert E. Lee, lined up to do endorsements.

(By the way—Mother must have known exactly what she was doing. For a while I tried to substitute yams for grits, but they weren't nearly bland enough on the way up. Too much acid for the esophagus!)

October 1, 1862

*D*ear Diary,

Today Doc Meade asked me to go home and not look after the sick soldiers anymore.

"You're just the worst nurse I've ever seen, honey child. You depress our men."

"Why, whatever do you mean," I replied. "Don't I sing to them all the time?"

"Your songs give them nightmares!" he yelled. "Get out of here!"

Well, Diary, I never! I try to sing songs that our boys will like, and I set them to tunes they know. I'll let you be the judge. Here's one, to the tune of "Dixie."

Oh, I wish that I didn't really feel so rotten
My leg's blown off and I've been shotten
Go away, go away, go away
Mr. Death . . .

Now, wouldn't that cheer you up, Diary?

November 2, 1862

$\mathscr{D}$ear Diary,

Had a terrible nightmare last night, woke up screaming. I dreamt that over a hundred years from now, Ashley would be the most popular girls' name in America, and that little female babies would also be named Tara. Isn't that queer?

November 12, 1862

$\mathcal{D}$ear Diary,

Our darkies continue to amaze me. Here they are pretending not to be able to read, and today I found a copy of one of their magazines, *SLAVE!*, out in the outhouse. I was going to get angry that one of them was using my john, but then the magazine was sooooooo interesting that I forgot to do anything about it. There was a really good article, "The Seven Habits of Highly Defective Masters," and a swell advice column, "Ask Harriet." A couple of the letters sounded familiar, though. Like this one:

Dear Harriet,

My mistress lies, cheats, and marries men for money, but she seems okay. Her hobbies include humiliating other men's wives, making clothes out of curtains, and running lumber mills. Here's my question: Should I tell her that there is one very handsome man who loves her completely, and that she could be totally happy if she would just get off her high horse and stop acting like a total bitch, or should I enjoy watching her ruin her life?

Love Slave

Dear Love Slave,

At least she has a life to ruin, and you should get one too, sister! Let the white oppressor figure out dating for herself.

November 26, 1862

*D*ear Diary,

Big excitement here in Atlanta. Hugh Grant, General Grant's son, was found in the back of a buggy getting his pickle licked. The newspaper says he was caught with a lady of ill repute as they were parked in front of a general store up in Utica. I gave an interview saying she was one of my girls I sent up North to work for the Cause in mysterious ways!

August 25, 1864

*D*ear Diary,

The siege of Atlanta and fear and privations are getting to everyone. From one day to the next we don't know whether or what we will eat, whether we will have a roof over our heads, or which dear childhood friend will appear on the lists of the dead or arrive grievously wounded at the hospital. I thought even Pa, my pillar of strength, was cracking under the strain. A letter from him arrived today inquiring, "How is Wade?" Wade who? I thought. How the hell should I know the current status of some fool Wade character? I even said to Melanie, "Melly, my daddy is wacko. He's asking about imaginary people." "Why, whatever do you mean, Scarlett, honey?" Melly asked in that treacly way of hers. So I told her about Pa's psychotic letter. "Have you ever met any Wade, Melly?" "Why, Scarlett, dear, can you possibly have forgotten that Wade is your son by poor dear dead Charles?"

Was my face red. I *had* forgotten. Now that she reminded me I remembered that old saying, "Forget and forgive," which I had pretty near been able to do. Frankly, the way I was brought up, southern gentlemen are not expected to pee and poop all over the place and then expect the ladies to clean up after them, so his behavior had really never earned him a very high place on *my* dance card. Still, I did try to remember where I had last seen young Wade, and what he looked like, but I just couldn't. Maybe, I suggested, he got called off with the old men and other young boys of the Home Guard to join General Hood in his last desperate defense of Atlanta. Just the sort of thing young Wade *would* have done, I said, thinking that's what that chump Melly would want to hear. He's such a hero, I said, just like his father, who would have whupped them Yankees good if he hadn't died of measles before he got out of training camp. "Now Scarlett, dear," Melanie said, "you know Wade is only two years old. Why, you celebrated his birthday just two months ago." I covered as best I could, pretending it had been a joke, but even Melly seemed doubtful. Well, at least that was a clue. So I had seen him two months ago. . . . But where had he gone since? How would he have gotten there? I can't remember, can two-year-olds walk or ride horses? Ah, well, some mysteries will never be solved. I wish young Wade Hamilton well, wherever he may be. I give him a mother's blessing.

EDITOR'S NOTE: This entry demonstrates Scarlett O'Hara's lifelong propensity to ignore, misplace, and forget her children and other accessories like scarves and gloves. In fact, scholars have variously estimated the total number of Scarlett's children as anywhere from three to nine.

$\mathscr{D}$ear Diary,

Whoops! I think I started something I didn't mean to. The pesky Rhett Butler came around again, saying how hot he is for me. We were standing near the stable out back and he was trying to feel me up. "C'mon baby, light my fire," he said, with that ridiculous twinkle in his eye. "I'll light your fire, you mustachioed beef jerky!" I screamed, and then struck a match under his boot to try to give him a hotfoot. Well, there was a lot of straw all around, and before you knew it, the fire was spreading all over Atlanta. The best I can do now is blame it on Sherman and his damn Yankees. Rhett thought it was hilarious and immediately left to corner the market on wienies and marshmallows. That man has an eye for business, that's for sure.

In the meantime, Diary, I've got to round up the whole damn dysfunctional family and get them in a wagon to go back to Tara. Melanie is upstairs moaning and groaning with that stupid newborn of hers. If you ask me, she's carrying this postpartum depression stuff a little too far. Mammy is a great midwife, and just because she got carried away with that underwater birth routine and nearly drowned Melanie at one point is not any excuse for all this moping around. (Besides, she should be relieved—Prissy was yakking away with that horrible voice of hers, and Mammy told her to check underwater to see how things were going. Then she held down that squeaky little slave's noggin until she bubbled. Now she seems to have lost her voice.)

Diary, I have to stop now. Mammy has run into the room in an asbestos suit. "Damn those O'Learys and their clumsy cow! They done set the whole place on fire. I thought they moved to Chicago last week!"

PART III

From Hunger

The Struggles at Tara

With Atlanta burned to the ground and damn Yankees swarming over the ruins, Scarlett's thoughts turned back to Tara. Not knowing whether the beloved old plantation still stood or not, she made her way through the ravaged countryside in search of peace and familiar faces.

November 21, 1864

$\mathcal{D}$ear Diary,

It's my first night back at Tara, and my heart is breaking. I could accept just about anything those damn Yankees did—they took all our crops, our livestock, our jewelry, silver, and china. Nevertheless, there was one thing I was looking forward to at my homecoming that has been robbed from me forever. "Now, Katie Scarlett, you must brace yourself for the worst blow of all," said Pa as we sat over whiskey last night. "General Sherman rode through here, and he took quite a shine to that little dog of yours. I'm afraid he ordered his aides to scoop him up and bring him along with the troops to the sea."

"Not Mr. Peabody!" I said, bursting into sobs.

"Aye, my dear girl. Sherman took your little pooch Mr. Peabody away forever."

"That human dog!" I said, spitting into the fire. "Mr. Peabody is twice the man he is!" Later, as I wandered around the plantation by moonlight pulling up radishes, gobbling them, and then puking, I looked down at one of the radish clumps and saw the tiny pair of glasses my nearsighted canine friend always wore. I hope Sherman is humane enough to read the newspaper to the little fellow.

November 27, 1864

*D*ear Diary,

I shot a Yankee today, right clear through his ugly head. He had twenty dollars in gold, a wad of greenbacks, a bunch of stolen jewelry, and a horse. I buried him under the scuppernong arbor while Melanie mopped up the blood. A month ago the idea of killing anyone, even a Yankee, would have horrified me, but now I find it kind of neat. Fiddle-dee-dee. Melly did pretty well. The girl shows promise.

November 28, 1864

*D*ear Diary,

Melly and I rode the dead Yankee's horse over to a disgusting tavern, got drunk, and danced all night. To protect our sacred families' names we called ourselves Selma and Louise. As we were about to remount and ride home some damn Yankee tried to rape me out back, so Melly shot him in a very interesting place. She was so intoxicated by the experience that she wanted us to go on a crime spree and then ride the horse off a cliff at the end, just to make a big splash. *That* would give those Mitchells something to write about!

November 29, 1864

𝒟ear Diary,

At sunset, we met the cutest little Yankee hitchhiker by the side of the road. Melly was riding sidesaddle and he jumped up behind her. We stopped for the evening and the two of them disappeared for a long time. From the sounds they made back behind the bushes later, I don't think she'll ever ride sidesaddle again.

November 30, 1864

𝒟ear Diary,

Goddammit! That cute hitchhiking Yankee stole all our silver and jewelry we'd been pilfering. Melly is wandering around cross-eyed, moaning about how a man never made her feel that way before. Makes me think twice about Ashley, that's for sure. "Well, I hope you enjoyed your little roll in the weeds, honeychile," I said. "Just remember how you swooned when you're eating maggots next month!"

December 1, 1864

𝒟ear Diary,

Shot two more Yankees today and buried them under the arbor. Fiddle-dee-dee. I guess those scuppernong grapes won't need fertilizing this year.

December 2, 1864

𝒟ear Diary,

Shot four Yankees today using only two bullets. Fiddle-dee-dee. Melly says she's getting tired of mopping up the blood. I offered to shoot her, too, but she pointed out that then *I* would have to clean up, so I gave in and swore off murder for the time being. God's nightgown!

December 15, 1864

𝒟ear Diary,

Got a new idea for a book today. Bet it would be a bestseller, especially if I could get someone to illustrate it, kind of like a cartoon book. I've started jotting down ideas:

101 Uses for a Dead Yankee

- Put 'em against the door to keep out drafts

- Use their jaws for cracking hickory nuts

- Boil them up for soup stock

- Throw 'em in the Slatterys' well to poison the drinking water

- Cut 'em into bait for catfish

- Put lanterns in their hands and use them as lawn ornaments

I've got to work on this, Diary. Maybe if I kill more Yankees, the ideas will come.

January 12, 1865

*D*ear Diary,

Heard a shot today and looked up—one of the Fife twins had been duck hunting and shot down two men in a hot air balloon. Those boys have ham hocks for brains! Fortunately, the man and his little assistant were all right, just startled. The big one, a handsome devil, started jabbering at me right away in what sounded like French. I sent Prissy to get the Tarletons' cook, Jean-Luc Picard, so we could figure out who they were.

January 14, 1865

*D*ear Diary,

That wonderful Frenchman's name is Jules Verne. He's traveling with his assistant, Jacques. Jean-Luc came over and translated for us, although Jules and I are already communicating through heavy body language. Seems he's checking facts on a book he wrote, *Around the World in Eighty Days.* But who cares what he'll write? The man can cook, and he can kiss real good. He sent his balloon over to Atlanta to be repaired, so he'll be here for a while. In the meantime, he's kicked Aunt Jemima out of the kitchen, and he's got Prissy out hunting frogs—says he's going to make us some frogs' legs.

January 20, 1865

*D*ear Diary,

Little Jacques has taken a shine to Mammy/Phillipe, and they've gone off on a romantic weekend to Charleston together. I'm happy—it's the first person Mammy has taken a cotton to since Mother died. Jules—oh, I could say his name over and over again, Jules, Jules, Jules!—is showing me some of the finer European romantic techniques. Vive la France!

January 23, 1865

𝒟ear Diary,

Much too exhausted to write. . . . Jules and I haven't gotten out of bed for days, except to nibble at some foie gras he made from the Slatterys' goose. . . . Ooh la la.

February 5, 1865

𝒟ear Diary,

Jules and Jacques left today. I cried piteously, but he just kept telling me to remember that there's no place like home and handed me a pair of ruby red shoes as they took off in the hot air balloon. He was babbling in French, and Jean-Luc translated again. Seems that Jules was saying that his next stop was Kansas, and that in his absence he appointed our scarecrow to be the ruler of Tara. I don't know what he was talking about, but I guess writers hit the sauce pretty hard.

February 6, 1865

𝒟ear Diary,

I am just desperate for money! If I don't do something soon, I'll have to sell Tara. But today I got an idea—what do you think? Since all the horses are dead and it's hard to get around, maybe I could start selling things through the mail. I started noting down cute ideas:

KLAN'S END CATALOG, featuring 100% white cotton sheets pre-cut for your convenience. Order the sheets that keep their shape, night ride after night ride!

BURY EVERYTHING! The catalog with creative ideas for hiding stuff from the Yankees. You never know when you'll have to bury all your valuables. Next time it happens, do it in style. Our catalog features the best in underground storage—fake stumps, anthills, rocks, and other exciting places to stash away jewels, silver, and other heirlooms. And our faux root cellar sells for only $89.95 (sorry, Confederate money not accepted).

SCARLETT'S SECRET, offering unmentionables made out of the finest draperies and lace curtains. Silky boxer shorts for ladies and exciting split-crotch lace bikinis made from exotic Belgian curtains. Try our new Miracle Bustle—it contains a hidden compartment so you can keep all your internal organs in an outside pouch. Your waist looks slimmer than ever, and your intestines aren't constricted.

Well, I'm sure going to try this idea soon. Until then, Diary, just remember: Tomorrow is another shopping day.

February 8, 1865

$\mathcal{D}$ear Diary,

I just love cotton, don't you? Today I got two great new ideas for our crop. I was fiddling around with some little tufts of the fluffy stuff and some matchsticks, and I came up with this nifty doodad to clean your ears. I tried it on Suellen and the sticks broke off down near her eardrum, but I'm sure I can figure out a way to make them safer. Suellen died of a terrible infection, so I'll name them Su-Tips after her.

As for my other invention—well, I got to thinking of all the things that are made of cotton. There's material, for instance, and rags are made out of material, right? And I hate wearing rags every month when I'm bleeding. So I thought, what if I could make something out of cotton that women could wear *inside* their bodies? I combed and rolled up some cotton real tight—I think it was only about five or six inches thick—and I tried it on Tampaxa, one of the darkies who just started her period. I don't know how it's going to work. First of all she screamed something fierce when I was trying to get it up her, and now I notice she's kind of waddling around. Oh well, back to the drawing board.

February 9, 1865

$\mathcal{D}$ear Diary,

Now that all the real southern gentlemen have been killed, their families driven off, plantations burned, the poor white trash are getting awfully uppity. The Slattery family has been putting on airs. But the worst are those Benettons. With their two acres of cotton fields they say they are going to start their own country, the United Colors of Benetton, selling earth-tone dickies to Northerners. I never!

February 11, 1865

*D*ear Diary,

I do declare, I don't know how it started, but Melanie and I got into a terrible row yesterday. I suppose it's the boredom, with no men around and nothing happening. It's been raining for a fortnight now, and this morning Melly and I were sitting at breakfast when I innocently took the last pat of butter for my grits. Well, Melly just reared up and challenged me to a fight.

"Let's go outside, Scarlett, honey," she said. "I want to whup the living daylights out of you."

So we went out to the front drive, where it was getting pretty soggy, and Melly jumped on me right away. I fell into a puddle, and soon we were both covered with a whole layer of mud.

"Take off your clothes," yelled Pork, the house Negro, who seemed to really be enjoying our altercation.

I thought that made a lot of sense, so I stripped, and so did Melly, and we slipped and slid all over that front yard. Melly took hold of my hair, and I grabbed her locket with Ashley's picture in it.

A couple of Yankees stopped by, and Pork told them it would be five dollars if they wanted to stay and see the mud wrestling. What quick thinking! Pork collected a cool twenty dollars and later insisted on keeping ten percent of the "gate," while Melly and I continued to gain fame as our county's only female mud-wrestlers. Pork told me that after the war he wanted to become a fighting impresario. Lately he's taken to combing his hair straight up on his head, and he spends a lot of time with the other Negroes scouting for wrestling and boxing champions.

February 15, 1865

𝒟ear Diary,

I am bored to tears back here at Tara. Nothing to do, no place to go. Nobody feels like dancing anymore, what with the South crushed and all and most everyone dead anyway. To amuse myself I started reading up on things, science mostly, to see if I can invent something that might make us some money.

February 17, 1865

*D*ear Diary,

This afternoon some funny-talking foreign gentleman passed through town. I struck up a conversation with him because he looked kind of cute and could have been fun but wasn't. While we were talking, Mammy came storming out, furious because she whipped up a mountain of buckwheat cakes and then discovered that the milk had gone sour. This man, Mr. Pasteur, said it always puzzled him "why zee milk he does turn sow-wair." I told him about my hunch that milk is full of tiny creatures, and that if we heat it up for a while we'll kill them and the milk won't go bad so quickly. I was thinking of experimenting with this process, which I call O'Harization. He said this was a foolish idea, and that a pretty thing such as myself should not worry her little head with such ideas, though he would be amused to hear any others I might have. I told him my idea for a rabies vaccine, which he also found preposterous. It's good that men are around to keep our flighty female fancies in check.

February 19, 1865

*D*ear Diary,

An itinerant telegrapher came to the door asking for a drink of water. I was happy to meet someone who knew about electricity, as I was having a little trouble in my studies. I told him about my ideas for a light bulb, phonograph, and motion picture camera. He seemed very confused and said he couldn't understand how you would get music from a light bulb or why a moving camera would take better pictures than one that stayed still, but he took lots of notes, said he had enjoyed our conversation, and promised to send me a postcard from his home in Menlo Park.

February 22, 1865

𝒟ear Diary,

It certainly has gotten busy around here, though such a pack of useless people I have never seen. A Mr. Alex Bell and a foreigner, Tony Marconi, came to Tara. We all asked if they had news of the war, but they didn't. What a shame, I said, that there isn't something better than the telegraph for communicating over long distances, maybe something that could link each individual home with the rest of the world. "Haw, haw, my green-eyed vixen," chortled Mr. Bell, while his nasty little friend sneaked behind me and pinched my thigh, "and just how would you propose to do that?" I said I thought you could modify the telegraph to transmit voices electrically from one house to another. Or I could imagine that voices could be sent long distances through the air by means of invisible light rays. Tony Marconi said that was the stupidest thing he had ever heard, and that he couldn't wait to tell his son Guglielmo, who loves a good joke.

February 24, 1865

*D*ear Diary,

I had a dream that some extremely heavy mineral exists that will explode when large quantities of it are squeezed tightly together. If the South possessed the technology of my dream, we could have destroyed northern cities, such as Harrisburg and Narragansett, intimidating the Yankees with our might and bringing a mercifully quicker end to the war.

February 25, 1865

*D*ear Diary,

This morning I drew up plans for a solid fuel rocket that would enable us to leave Georgia completely and establish a new Confederate colony on the moon or Mars or some other planet. But Pork and Mammy say they are house niggers, not aerospace niggers, so they refused to help out, and that damn fool sister of mine Careen was afraid she would get freckles or blisters working out on the launch pad, and Prissy drives me bonkers with her whining and that weird voice of hers, so I gave up the whole plan. I've had it with science and invention. I think I'll just go back to sex and mindless femininity.

March 1, 1865

𝒟ear Diary,

As God is my witness, I'll never go hungry again. Not as long as I keep clipping these great recipes from Miss Yummy Yum's Wartime Feast column in the *Tara Times*. Why, I can scrape together a whole meal out of practically nothing! We had a great dinner tonight, so I'll paste in the clippings for keeps.

Buggy Ride Dinner for Eight

Well, ladies, it's deeeeelicious bug-harvesttime once again, and Miss Yummy Yum has put together a meal bound to stir a buzz and get your evening off to a flying start.

Cicada Soup

Ingredients:
- *3 quarts boiling water*
- *25 cicadas*

Crush cicadas with a stone, then add to other ingredients. Cook for twenty minutes, stirring, until it thickens. (Note: It should be the texture and color of healthy snot.) Serve immediately with lawn grass garnish in each bowl.

Old McDonald's Earthworm Sushi Appetizer

This recipe works best with meaty night crawlers. Stun the critters with a toothpick, empty their bowels, and serve immediately with rock salt or, if available, soy or hot sauce.

Stuffed Boll Weevil Fajitas

Ingredients:
- *A dozen big leaves of any kind*
- *Three dozen boll weevils, minced*
- *Pinch of flour, salt, and pepper*

Combine minced boll weevils with spices, place a heaping tablespoon of the mixture on the side of each leaf, and roll, tucking in the ends. Roast in fireplace or over open fire for twenty minutes or until crispy. Serve with salamander salsa if available.

March 6, 1865

$\mathscr{D}$ear Diary,

Did you ever notice how, when girls live together, they start getting their time of the month during the same week? Now that Melanie and I have been under the same roof for years, everybody knows to clear out the week before the redcoats are coming.

Not that I'm that bad. I just scream and yell a lot and hit the brandy jug too much a day or two before I go on the rag. Melanie is a whole different story. Right before she commences her menses, Melly starts resembling a mountain lion in heat who's got a thorn in her paw and a poker up her ass. Why, you could almost call what the Divine Miss M goes through a syndrome or something. I talked to Ashley about it once, and he agreed, and even Mammy had to admit that she's found Little Miss Perfect Wife gobbling down bags of her homemade sweet-potato chips out in the pantry whenever the curse is about to come upon her.

The whole lunatic process seems to take about seven days, so last month I decided to jot down a few notes about the pre-menses Melly, just to prove to everybody that she's not always the saint she's cracked up to be.

DAY #1

Found Melly in her room trying on every outfit she owns. When I asked what was the matter, she yelled, "I'm fat, I'm fat and disgusting!" "But Melanie," I said. "You weigh ninety-five pounds!" Then she burst into tears and accused me of stealing three of her favorite blouses.

DAY #2

Tonight, when he went out to water what's left of the livestock, Daddy found Melanie naked, howling at the moon and tonguing the salt lick out in the western cornfield. I told him she was doing it on a dare from the women's reading club.

DAY #3
Poor Beau. He went upstairs to ask his mom if he could go out and play, and she accidentally cut off his ear with her sewing scissors.

DAY #4
Melanie shot what she claimed were two Yankees out her bedroom window. Turns out it was the local priest, Father Flanagan, and his altar boy. She fell to pieces, so naturally yours truly had to dig the graves. And I have cramps too!

DAY #5
Heard muffled sounds of distress and a cracking sound coming from Melanie's room. After Mammy dismantled the lock, we burst in on a strange scene. There was Ashley, home on leave, blindfolded, bound and gagged at the bedpost, and little Miss Melly standing over him with a horsewhip. She turned and threatened to use it on us, too, if we came any farther, so we stayed a while and watched. Damn, she has great technique for a tiny thing!

DAY #6
Melanie came down to breakfast all sweetness and light, humming and promising to needlepoint us each a special coverlet. Guess some blood other than Ashley's finally started flowing. Ashley said he didn't have "time" to sit down at the table. At least he has a whole 'nother month to heal.

March 18, 1865

$\mathscr{D}$ear Diary,

I know it's been a while since I've written, but I've been gone for over a week. Melanie won't listen to anything that happened to me. Says I have a fever and I've been hallucinating. Mammy and Prissy just claim I got into the corn whiskey and went on a bender. But I know that something really happened, so I'm going to do my best to reconstruct the events.

Heard some rustling in the kitchen last Tuesday night. "Aha!" I thought. "Those damn Yankees are back again. I'll teach them to come snoopin' around Tara." Crept down the backstairs with my shotgun cocked, and there were three little hairless green men smelling the rutabagas and sticking long bony fingers into Mammy's apple pie. Knew right away they were no Yankees, unless they were from even farther up north than I'd ever heard about.

Before I knew what hit me, the biggest one had turned some sort of light on me and I couldn't move. They picked me up by my cute little waist and carried me out the door. I tried to scream, but when I opened up my mouth no sound came out. They took me out behind the barn, where I saw a beautiful big disk—looked like Jules's hot air balloon, only a lot bigger. Another beam of light came down from the disk, and before I knew it we were up inside the thing and I was tied to an examination table. Let me tell you, they did things to me that old Doc Meade never even dreamed of. They gave me a thorough going-over under the bustle, if you know what I mean. For days they probed me and prodded me and tried feeding me all sorts of things. And even though I never understood their language, I could read their minds. The big one from the kitchen really fell in love with me, and I started finding him pretty darn attractive too, even though I didn't know where his people were from or how many acres he owned up there on whatever planet he came from.

Yes, Diary—it's true! I think I really was kidnapped by men from another planet. But it wasn't no white trash planet—they were gentlemen, all right. Just curious gentlemen. In the end I let them all mate with me, seeing as I could read their minds and they kept thinking how they liked my green eyes and how they would want to colonize Earth by using my fine O'Hara lineage. They were kind and gentle, Diary—I think they might be the only men who have ever truly understood me. I tried to talk them into settling at Tara, working the land. Imagine how good at possum-hunting they'd be with those stun guns of theirs!

It was kind of nice. The last night I was there, or at least I think it was the last night, they made me one of their special dinners of flavor crystals, and I cooked them some hominy in a funny kind of oven that never really got hot but cooked food so darn fast you could hardly believe it. Then they took me for a joyride all around the sky, and it was wonderful. We were floating inside their space disk—I felt like I didn't weigh a thing, light as a feather. Being weightless sure opens up the possibilities for romance. I wish I could remember more, but the next thing I knew I was back in my bed, passed out, all sore in different parts of my body. "Get up, you worthless slut!" Mammy was screaming, and I began babbling in what she says sounded like another language. My tongue felt thick and swollen. I tried to show her a tiny tattoo with a weird symbol that my little green men had left on my behind, but Mammy just said I had probably been cavorting with drunken sailors. I went back to sleep and dreamed about a strange card game the little guys taught me, but then when I woke up I had forgotten how to play it.

Help me, Diary—I can't stop thinking about this experience. I wonder if they were really Yankee spies and they did it all with mirrors. But maybe they were real. Maybe they'll come back again for me, and I won't ever have to be hungry again. If only I could give birth to a new race of superior southern belles—that would show Melanie and Mammy and Prissy, if I had a daughter whose green skin matched her eyes!

March 19, 1865

$\mathcal{D}$ear Diary,

Just found a strange little metal thing stuck in my skull, and I've noticed that whenever I try to remember what happened up there in the sky, I get a terrible piercing pain all over my brain. Oh well, at least I have a few hats left that will cover up the wires.

PART IV

Quickies

The Husband Years

To save Tara, which the Yankees were threatening to take for back taxes, Scarlett moved to Atlanta and married the dull Frank Kennedy, onetime suitor of the late Suellen O'Hara. Scarlett took surprisingly well to marriage—indeed, she wanted more and more of it.

April 10, 1865

𝒟ear Diary,

That Ashley Wilkes seems determined to drive me crazy. First it was his homosexual affair with Rhett, then his heterosexual marriage with Melly, and now it's an incestuous fling with his cousin John, some big-deal actor. They spend all their time together nuzzling and cuddling. It's enough to make you puke.

April 14, 1865

𝒟ear Diary,

I thought I had a great plan, but somehow it went wrong. Ashley and John planned to go to the theater in Washington together tonight. Their big cultural getaway. I knew that if Ashley were only given the chance he would realize that it had always been me, me, me, me that he loved. So I slipped cousin John Wilkes Booth a Mickey, just like my daddy taught me to make, dressed myself up in his clothes, and went to Ford's Theater with Ashley.

Well, the evening went fine until intermission. Then when I was downstairs having a drink or three, I saw Ashley lure some young usher into our box. I knew what he was up to. So I rushed back up, whipped out a pistol, burst through the door, yelled, "You sick, simpering jack-ass," and shot what I thought was the usher in the head.

How embarrassing. I accidentally went into President Lincoln's box. Fortunately, I was disguised as Ashley's cousin. People reported that I had yelled, "Sic semper tyrannis" and was a political assassin. They eventually caught John and killed him, which eliminated the competition, and I am proud to have anonymously served the Cause by bumping off Lincoln, selfless person that I am, but Ashley still eludes my grasp. Oh, well, tomorrow is another day.

October 26, 1865

$\mathscr{D}$ear Diary,

I was coming home from the lumber mill this afternoon and who rode up but Rhett Butler himself. Nobody has seen him in over three months, but here he rode up on his black stallion, dressed in all his immaculate finery, saying hello as if it were the most natural thing in the world for us to meet. "Well, Rhett Butler, where have you been? Off gallivanting about with Belle Watling, I presume?" "Oh, no, Scarlett, much worse than that. I won't tell you." "I suppose you've been consorting with scalawags and rapscallions and carpetbaggers and vacuum cleaners and their ilk." "No, Scarlett, not this time. Nor chimney sweeps, either." "So where have you been, Rhett?" "All right, I'll tell you the truth. Have you ever wondered why I talk so much? Why I'm so god-awful full of myself, and love to criticize you and preach about right and wrong and sneer at your lack of classical education?" "Yes I have, Rhett. That's the most unbearable thing about you." "Well, Scarlett, in my secret life I am a college professor. I teach undergraduate philosophy courses at a small liberal arts college up North. So I can only profiteer and run blockades and womanize and fraternize with the enemy when I am not teaching classes and marking exams. Sad, isn't it?"

March 4, 1867

$\mathcal{D}$ear Diary,

Damn that Frank Kennedy! At first I thought he was just getting drunk and snoozing in front of the fire every night, waiting for television and professional sports to be invented. Then I discovered it wasn't Frank at all, but a scarecrow he put there when he donned his Klan outfit and went rampagin' across the countryside fighting for the honor and purity of the South. I guess that explains why I always wound up with a mouthful of straw after kissing him, and why he was more lively in bed. But now it turns out he never belonged to the Klan at all. They wouldn't let him in because of his pro-integration opinions. Frank just liked the clothes. His idea of protecting lily-white American womanhood was joining the toga parties at Belle Watling's.

April 1, 1867

*D*ear Diary,

I was cleaning my gun when Frank walked across the yard in his white outfit. Such an irresistible target. . . . Well, he was a nice enough fellow, all things considered, though he bored me to tears. What a dullard. The gun pulls just a fraction to the left; I should get the sights adjusted before I remarry. I only meant to shoot his glasses off as a joke. Frank never did have a sense of humor. At least he'll be the hit of the party at his funeral. I should buy him a new suit of clothing to match my latest sexy mourning gown.

Rhett is such a doll. He took Frank over by Belle Watling's, then shot Tommy Wellburn to make it look like they'd killed each other in a brawl over whores. Then he spread the rumor that this was just a cover-up when they'd really been off riding with the Klan. Rhett is so clever. I think he has what it takes to go into politics.

June 30, 1867

*D*ear Diary,

Today I was waiting for the coach to Charleston and I met the strangest man. He was sitting on a bench with a box of chocolates next to him, and he wanted to tell me everything about his life. The weird thing was, he kept saying that life was like a box of chocolates, but every time he offered me a chocolate, it was the same kind. Said his name was Forrest Gump.

Seems that whenever something exciting was happening in the war, ol' Forrest was there. Claims to have been at almost every battle and at Ford's Theater when President Lincoln was shot (but he must have been looking the other way). Says he sang with Jenny Lind and was Tom Thumb's best man. Says he wrote the original lyrics to "The Battle Hymn of the Republic." Even claims he gave Harriet Beecher Stowe the idea for *Uncle Tom's Cabin.* In spite of this, he was the most boring man I've ever met. Just about the only thing he had going for him was that name—I'm a sucker for a southern male with a stupid moniker. Still, I can't imagine that any girl would want to marry a man so stupid. I'm sure his line will stop right here.

October 12, 1867

𝒟ear Diary,

Oh, lordy, lordy! So much to buy and so little to buy it with. I look back at my life and see what a shambles it is. I married Charlie Hamilton out of spite, and all it got me was a warehouse in Atlanta that burned to the ground, and that damned baby. I thought I was more clever marrying old Frank Kennedy, but all he did was pay the taxes on Tara, run his stupid store, complain about my lumber mill, and give me another damned baby. Now here I am widowed again. I need a husband. This time I'll do it right.

October 16, 1867

*D*ear Diary,

Mammy helped me make a new dress out of venetian blinds, which I can flip open or shut depending on the company. She thought a triple-track storm window and screen bodice would add a devastatingly exciting touch, but I vetoed the suggestion and said I would wear the shutters only if the weather turned bad. The caulk around the neck and sleeves itches, and I think it makes me look cheap.

October 17, 1867

*D*ear Diary,

Met the perfect man at the ball this evening. I guess the old window treatment worked again. George is ninety-two years old, bald, toothless, mildly retarded, and tends to drool, but he is *fabulously* rich, having inherited his father's patent medicine and soft drink company. He couldn't dance with me, of course, because he has no legs, but we sat together on the sofa and I shouted conversationally into his ear while he drank his mint julep and buttermilk through a straw. I think I could grow to love him. I am fairly certain he adores me, though with that stutter and his feeble command of the English language I may have misunderstood a word here and there.

October 18, 1867

$\mathscr{D}$ear Diary,

George has heirs. I fear this may harm our relationship. I like my men to be totally devoted to me, especially when money is involved.

October 20, 1867

$\mathscr{D}$ear Diary,

Poor George is so upset. He reminds me a bit of my father toward the end. Sometimes George believes that his family is still alive, and then when he remembers he simply cannot understand how it happened. I pat him on the hand and say the world twirls in mysterious ways. "But all twelve of them burned to death together, inside that barn with the lock on the outside?" he asked me. His tired old mind, so set in its ways, is unable to keep up with the changing times.

October 23, 1867

*D*ear Diary,

My darling George is a bit obtuse. I demurely fluttered my eyelids at him for the better part of an hour. Nothing. I told him he makes me feel positively faint with longing. "For what?" he asked. I said, "Oh, a gentleman shouldn't have to ask that of a lady," pouting and batting my eyes some more, but it all went clean over the old goat's head. Finally I ripped the front of my dress open and dangled my voluptuous breasts in front of his face. He gazed upon them for the longest time, then said, "Your skin makes me think of magnolias, Scarlett. I've always liked magnolias. Would you take me out in my chair to see magnolias sometime?"

Men!

October 25, 1867

*D*ear Diary,

Tough times call for drastic measures. George was slumped unconscious on the ground. At first I was afraid he was already dead, but he jerked when I stuck a pin in him. I shouted in his ear as loud as I could, "Why, yes, *yes,* George my darling. I will!" He stirred a bit and mumbled, "Huh?" "I will, George, I *will!*" "You will what?" he asked. "I will marry you, George. You proposed to me. Have you forgotten already? It was only twenty seconds ago!" I pouted and sobbed and wiped a tear from my eye, and of course being a southern gentleman, or at least the leftover pieces of one, he got all gallant and said he was mine forever. Bingo!

October 26, 1867

𝒟ear Diary,

Married George. I had to carry him up the aisle, but you know me and love—I will do whatever it takes. I pretended I was only coughing when I said ". . . till death do us part."

October 27, 1867

𝒟ear Diary,

Damn! How did he do it? I tucked George safely in bed at one end of the hall, then locked myself in my room with a large bottle of whiskey. But when I woke up this morning, there he was, in bed with me, stark naked. I think he did it.

November 4, 1867

𝒟ear Diary,

I haven't stopped crying since George fell down the stairs on his way to breakfast yesterday morning. My life is so wretched, filled with such misery. Still, I think a quick funeral is the best thing, so that one can get on with one's life, picking up the pieces, putting on the best face, settling that estate, shopping, shopping, shopping.

Some of my old pals came back to the house after the funeral, wanting to party. I told them they had a lot of nerve, with poor George dead less than a day and me still in mourning. Of course, tomorrow is another day.

July 4, 1867

𝒟ear Diary,

My darling George's baby was born today. I couldn't decide whether to give it one name, or whether each of the heads deserved a name of its own. I hear that some Yankee, Mr. P. T. Barnum, has a soft spot in his heart for nature's little idiosyncrasies, and will even pay for the honor of taking them under his wing. I will make sure the kid gets a good home.

PART V

The Butler Did It

The Rhett Years

After years of sexual frustration and prototype husbands, Scarlett finally married Rhett, the handsome bisexual scalawag, and they lived happily ever after for about forty-eight hours. This final installment of entries chronicles their troubled marriage and the changes in Scarlett's life and shape during her middle years. We also get a closer look at how the Mitchells misinterpreted Scarlett's adventures.

January 1, 1869

𝒟ear Diary,

I am so embarrassed! I shopped for weeks to find just the right silk nightgown for our wedding night, and then Rhett entered our suite wearing the exact same outfit! "I hope you don't mind, my dear, but I just adore fine garments," he said.

Well, Diary, I just don't like a man in fluffy clothes. All of a sudden I felt like I was kissing my sister with a moustache. Needless to say, it didn't go well. After waiting for Rhett all that time, I expected more. Instead, I found out he just really wanted to cuddle and swap stories about shoe shopping.

January 2, 1869

𝒟ear Diary,

Well, maybe I spoke too soon. Rhett got real masculine-like in the middle of the night, yelling, *"The South will rise again, the South will rise again!"* Of course, I resented the fact that he made me whistle "Dixie" all the time we were doing it, and then, when I got tired after about the eighth time, I hummed "The Battle Hymn of the Republic," and that brought him down.

January 8, 1869

*D*ear Diary,

I'm worried. Here I am only one week away on my honeymoon, and my new husband is obsessed with my mammy. He's even interested in her wardrobe. "I'll buy Mammy some red taffeta and have an elegant petticoat made," he says to me this morning. Oh boy, here we go. He must have some inkling that Mammy is not really Mammy—otherwise, why on earth would he think of *red* taffeta? Not exactly her color, do you think? And a gift of red lingerie might really unhinge poor Mammy/Phillipe. She—or he—has been so lonely since Mother died, a dainty little intimate like that might give her/him new ideas. Let's face it, too; Rhett's been known to swing both ways. Diary, am I stupid to be frettin' so on this?

November 28, 1869

*D*ear Diary,

Today I told Rhett I didn't want to have any more children. He thinks it's because I don't want to have sex with him. That's only part of it. Actually, sex with him *is* kind of messy—he leaves those terrible grease stains on the pillow from his slicked-back hair. But there are two more reasons why I don't want him poking me with his sausage anymore:

1. After Bonnie Blue was born, I ended up with a fifty-four-inch waist. Mammy and Prissy ordered a special hydraulic winch to lace me into one of those miracle corsets, and I still can only make it down to about thirty-two inches around the middle after they lace me up, so I'm looking at a lifetime sentence of vertical stripes. I don't think we have the corset technology to help me if I get knocked up again, and Rhett is always tricking me by leaving off the cotton condoms Melanie knits for me.

2. I found Rhett's baby-name book. Turns out he likes the name Bonnie Blue so much, he's decided to have a whole brood with nauseating monikers. He's written down Ritchie Red, Maggie Magenta, Tammy Turquoise, and Tommy Teal. Spare me!

December 13, 1869

$\mathcal{D}$ear Diary,

Good news! Mammy found out that one of the former slaves, Oprah, has a great new diet I can go on. Ever since I went over 350 pounds, I haven't been able to leave my room. But this Oprah girl tells me I *can* lose the weight by eating right. She introduced me to her cook friend, Rosie, who said she has great low-fat grit recipes and okra bran salads that will shape me up real good. Oprah wanted to know all about the weird things that have happened to me—said she's thinking of starting a series of stage shows about modern life, and asked if I would appear on the "Southern Belles Who Fall in Love with Extraterrestrials" segment. I said I would rather be one of those "I Was in Love With Two Men, and One of Them Was My Best Friend's Husband" type of gals. She wasn't interested in my racier topic, "I Shot Yankees in the Head and Then Had Sex With Them," because she said she doesn't do stuff like that anymore, but maybe I can get on her friend Montel's show. I guess I'll think about it.

February 3, 1870

$\mathscr{D}$ear Diary,

Rhett and I are still not getting along—it's pretty bad. I read in the *Southern Ladies' Home Journal* about this new kind of doctor, Doc Kinsey, who works with couples who can't communicate. Calls himself a marriage alienist. I called on him to see if he thinks he can help us.

"My work is based on the great married slave-owning romance specialists, the Masters of Johnson," he told me. "First I will talk to you and your husband—I call that counseling—and then I might even ask to sleep with one or both of you, or just to watch. I've helped scores of couples revive their flagging relationships."

"What's a relationship?" I asked.

"Ah. I see we'll have to start at the beginning. Bring your husband by tomorrow—"

"Tomorrow is another day!"

"Yes, I know that, Mrs. Butler."

February 5, 1870

𝒟ear Diary,

Rhett raised a real squawk when I told him where we were going. Said he might as well bring Belle Watling along too, since she's the one he's having sex with, but I put down my foot and told him we *had* to go or I would tell everyone about him and Ashley.

Actually, Diary, it was very interesting, even though Rhett just sat there most of the time with a sullen look on his face.

"Men are from Charleston, women are from Atlanta," said Doc Kinsey. Seems we speak a whole different dialect.

"It's like you're dancing at different cotillions," said the doc.

So I asked him: "Does that explain why Rhett wants to make love to me more than once or twice a year even though I'd rather eat a slice of pecan pie or just fondle my jewelry?"

"Hmm," said the doc. "Yes, I suppose it does."

Then, Diary, you could have knocked me on my bustle for what happened next. Rhett exploded!

"I am not attracted to this green-eyed little bitch any longer!" he screamed.

"And why not?" said the doctor in an even tone.

"It's the staircase thing. She can't seem to get excited unless I carry her up a very long flight of stairs, and it gets wearing. When we travel, she insists that I carry her up the hotel staircase. We're never allowed to stay on the first floor. I feel embarrassed. All that climbing is hard on my knees. I don't know how she can expect me to be full of lust for her right after I've hauled her pie-crust-lard derriere up sixty stairs."

"Oh, and I suppose Ashley and Mammy walked up the stairs by

themselves," I snarled. There was a moment of silence. The doctor looked a bit puzzled, but then he spoke.

"Scarlett, why are staircases so important to you during foreplay?"

"Oh, Doc, I don't know—when a man carries me up to my boudoir, I just feel like I'm on a stairway to heaven, you know? I want to feel swept off my feet. I need a man to *do* something for me."

"Yeah. You need a man to drop dead and leave you lots of money," said Rhett through clenched teeth.

"I'm sensing a lot of anger here," said the doc. "For our next session, I'd like you to take a look at my book, *Belles Who Marry Scalawags Who Love Whores Who Hate Belles Who Hate Scalawags Who Adore Belles.*"

"Why, doctor, whatever could that have to do with us?" I asked, batting my eyelashes.

Rhett got up to leave. "See you later, Scarlett. If you want me I'll be at Belle's."

February 11, 1870

*D*ear Diary,

I got so excited today because Rhett said he would do one of our marriage encounter exercises with me. You're supposed to blindfold the other person and then lead him or her around. It's all about developing trust in marriage. Rhett bought me a gorgeous green silk blindfold, and I was beginning to feel really warm toward him as he led me around town and then into what felt like a field. "Good-bye, my dear," he said abruptly, and then I heard the clicking of muskets. Good thing my reflexes are so good, 'cause I dropped to the ground. When I pulled my blindfold off I saw a Yankee firing squad facing me and Rhett talking with the commander, laughing.

February 21, 1870

𝒟ear Diary,

I am so upset. I told Doc Kinsey what happened, and he couldn't believe it. Rhett and I were making love, and he told me he would pull out, and he didn't. He just laughed. I guess he doesn't have to worry about ballooning up or supervising the slaves to take care of some little brat.

Doc Kinsey asked Rhett why he wouldn't withdraw, why he wouldn't attend to my needs for birth control. Rhett just got one of those big shit-eating grins on his face.

"Frankly, Doc, unlike most southerners, I never believed in secession."

March 7, 1870

𝒟ear Diary,

Consarn those white trash Mitchells! Mammy found one of them listening at the kitchen door, taking notes. Rhett discovered one of them under our bed! This evening we heard a weird tapping up near the roof, and it turned out little Miller Mitchell was hiding in the attic, listening through the ceiling with a stethoscope, sending dispatches on what we were saying in Morse code over a wire they'd strung across the lower pasture.

March 10, 1870

𝒟ear Diary,

Got the Mitchells interested in Forrest Gump's story, and I thought I was rid of them. "If you can make a novel out of this man's stupidity and fixation on shrimp, you can do anything," I promised. So they left. But then the county declared White Trash Recycling Day, and the Mitchells returned, nosy as ever.

June 17, 1871

𝒟ear Diary,

To save my life I can't figure out whether that Melanie is the dumbest southern belle on earth or whether she's so sainted good that she just seems dumb. She saw Ashley and me hugging in the pantry, and all she said was, "Oh, Ashley, how nice of you to keep Scarlett from falling down. And, Scarlett, how nice of *you* to keep *Ashley* from falling down." She walked in while I was humping Archie, that peg-legged ex-convict who used to drive me to the lumberyard, and she told India and Aunt Potty that I was nobly using my powerful thighs to extract an enormous splinter from his groin. When I clubbed that damned Slattery slut to death she went on for weeks about how, as the poor girl was dying of some unexplained brain damage, all I could think of was making her last moments more pleasant by getting rid of her head lice. And when I set fire to Atlanta, she wondered aloud how many other women would go to so much trouble just so that a small group of close friends could chat about old times while making themselves some S'mores.

April 3, 1872

𝒟ear Diary,

We stopped seeing Doc Kinsey because Rhett has turned into a real daddy-track scalawag. He doesn't drink, whore, or insult people anymore, which makes him very popular and a fine husband, but his business is suffering most dreadfully.

April 11, 1872

*D*ear Diary,

Rhett wants to give Bonnie Blue dolls and other such girlie stuff, but I want to teach her to love the land, the land, like my Irish pa taught me. So I gave her a moist red lump of rich Georgia soil. She ate it.

April 15, 1872

*D*ear Diary,

Beau, Ella, and Bonnie Blue have been playing very nicely together. That old peg-legged ex-convict ruffian Archie keeps them in line, but they all love him dearly because he has a heart of gold under that gruff homicidal exterior. Other moms have been asking if they can leave their kids with Archie too. I think I will start a day-care center. If you have kids, you might as well figure out a way to make money on them, I say. Rhett finds this hard-hearted of me. I say it's just practical. "What are children for, then?" I ask him, and he doesn't have an answer. If my day-care center does well, maybe I'll open another one and ask Ashley to run it. There must be something that man can do.

May 12, 1879

𝒟ear Diary,

Mammy and I had a long talk today while she was on break out back. She's taken to getting out of her Mammy suit and smoking cigars on the back stoop a couple of times a day. For as long as I've known her, it still startles me to see her as a thin white man.

"Scarlett, I know all this seems mighty peculiar to you, even after all these years," she said today, "but inside every black mammy there's a thin gentleman waiting to get out. In fact, I'm beginning to think that the black mammy herself is just an icon of oppression crafted by dominant white male oppressors as an expression of their guilt. I tell you, when you walk a million miles in that mammy suit, it changes your thinking about race and class in America forever. I'm thinking of writing a book.

"Yes. *Black Mammy Like Me,* that's what I'll call it. I'm sorry to have to tell you this, Scarlett, but I'm giving notice. I'm going up North to finish my law degree, and then I will campaign for civil rights."

"Oh Mammy," I sobbed, collapsing into her/his thin white arms. "I knew you weren't happy ever since you couldn't be my personal slave anymore!"

"You've got that right, girlfriend. But I will miss you, and Prissy, and definitely Mr. Rhett. He's one hell of a man, Scarlett—he certainly makes me swoon."

"But Mammy—you're a man!"

"Scarlett, when are you going to get over your gender fixation? Sexual identity is in constant flux, and we must learn to access both our feminine and masculine sides if we are to live as fully satisfied human beings."

That Mammy! I never did understand a word she said, especially after she started taking that correspondence course from Harvard.

November 29, 1879

*D*ear Diary,

Rhett seems to be losing his mind. He's been ranting and raving that the whores don't give him any respect now that he's turned into such a goody two-shoes. They always laugh when they see him doing the shopping or hanging up the laundry or doing all the other things Mammy used to do, especially when he wears her red taffeta petticoat and ties that kerchief around his head. Then on Thanksgiving he was carving the turkey when all of a sudden he just started screaming, "On your knees, Belle! Take *that*! and *that*! and *that*!"—and he began stabbing and slashing that poor bird until it was nothing but slivers.

December 2, 1879

*D*ear Diary,

Rhett says the whores are still teasing him. He sees them everywhere—hiding under the bed, in the outhouse, in his shoes. . . . They point and tell him he is Rhetticulous or Rhettarded or a Rhettched specimen of a man. Doc Meade says Rhett is deluded and that we should humor him, but this is difficult. Today Rhett said he was getting completely fed up with all these taunts, and thought maybe he should change his name, to something like Jack, maybe.

December 5, 1879

$\mathscr{D}$ear Diary,

All of Atlanta was shocked when five of Belle's whores were found eviscerated in an alley. I didn't want Rhett to hear about it, because he's been in such a touchy mood lately, but today he has been awfully cheerful—laughing, singing, and cutting up like his old fun-loving self. When Ashley came over and started talking about the murders, Rhett just giggled like a little girl. It didn't seem to bother him a bit.

December 7, 1879

$\mathscr{D}$ear Diary,

I'm glad Rhett is going to England for a while. I think the change of scene will do him a lot of good and give him the chance to get his mind off Belle Watling and her girls. He is doing much better, though he still does strange things from time to time. He says he is traveling incognito, and I should write him as Jack Butler at the Whitechapel Arms. Whatever makes him happy.

June 8, 1880

*D*ear Diary,

First Pa, then Bonnie Blue. Seems everybody in my family goes over a horse's ears sooner or later. I had a vision this evening of a wonderful invention—a bale of cotton fastened with a hinge and counterweight to the front of the horse. If the horse stops too suddenly, the cotton bale swings up to cushion the rider's fall. I've asked Pork to work up a prototype and take care of the patent application. If my invention is successful, I'll petition the Yankee government to meddle in our affairs some more and make these devices mandatory on every horse in the country by 1890.

August 22, 1880

*D*ear Diary,

Melly's dying again. She's like the girl who cried wolf—she's done it so many times, it's hard to take her seriously. Besides, she's made money out of it. Her book, *What to Expect When You're Expiring,* has sold millions of copies, and now she and Ashley are building a big house by the ocean.

"Scarlett, honey," she said to me last time she was on her so-called deathbed. "I walked down a wonderful corridor of light, and there were lots of folks there to greet me. Why, I saw your mama and papa and Charlie, my brother and your first husband, and Frank, your second husband, and George, your third husband, and Rhett, your fourth husband. . . ."

"But Rhett's not dead yet!" I cried.

"Oh. Well, maybe he was right here in the room with me. I go between the two worlds so much, I get confused."

"So did you see any of those Yankees we rubbed out?" I asked, getting annoyed.

"Now, Scarlett, you know where they would be! Really, the afterworld is such a beautiful place. You should try it. Just get yourself knocked up and fall down the stairs—you'll love nearly dying."

Well, Diary, I tried it, and it never worked for me. All I ever saw when I nearly croaked were those Mitchells hanging around trying to catch my last breath. I think I might have seen the Tarleton twins sneaking down a lighted corridor, but they were busy trying to look up my dress.

Anyhow, isn't it just like Melanie to take something like death and make it seem all nice and pretty? Now that she's supposedly kicking the bucket yet again, there are hundreds of people hanging around for her "workshop"—they're watching her eyelids flutter and taking notes on every little moan she makes. I know she's faking it, just the way Ashley always said she faked certain other things.

August 23, 1880

𝒟ear Diary,

So call me a liar. Melly really is pushing up daisies—she slipped away last night, all the while mumbling about embracing the light. At least Ashley can live off her royalties. He hired some carpetbagger who calls himself a "public relations adviser," and they decided to bury

Melanie under the scuppernong grape arbor and just pretend she's still alive and on an extended book tour.

November 4, 1880

𝒟ear Diary,

Those Mitchell folks are getting awfully annoying lately. They must work for the *National Enquirer* or something, always snooping around, sifting through the trash, listening at keyholes, peering through windows, following us everywhere we go and jotting down notes. This afternoon I was sitting on the steps having a perfectly pleasant conversation with Rhett, when I noticed one of *those* folks with her ear stuck up against the crack of the door. I was tempted to take a buggy whip to her, but Rhett and I were having such a grand time, joking back and forth, planning where we should go for our second honeymoon, that I just couldn't be bothered. Just then Frank Lee, one of the stable boys from around the corner, came in through the back way. Seems Frank and Rhett once had a little thing going. That's fine with me. But now that the scalawags and carpetbaggers are being driven out, young Frank, Yankee lover that he was, thought he should get out of town, and he'd come to beg some money off of Rhett. "If you don't give me what I want, Rhett, I'll tell the whole world about our relationship." Rhett drew himself up tall and proud and said, "Frank Lee, my dear, I don't give a damn." I noticed that Mitchell woman scribbling furiously just then. She seemed to enjoy that line for some reason. Rhett and I had a great laugh.

[NOTE: At this point, the diary's pages are severely damaged. We were able to read several fragments, which indicate that Scarlett had another rather unusual encounter before disappearing from the public eye.]

. . . and they sent down the ladder, and there was the little green one I had called Henry, the one who did all those sexy things with that medical probe. He waved to me, inviting me on board again. He had something in his hand—Diary, I couldn't believe it! The little guy had landed in Paris just to get me a new bonnet. I made him come down here to give it to me, though. He brought along a whole crew, and they hauled something down the ladder toward the house. Looked like an icebox of some sort . . .

. . . seems like a good idea. I'm sick of Georgia, and now that Bonnie Blue is gone, Rhett has stopped doing the laundry and gone back to his whoring and gambling. It would sure make him jealous to know I went off with another man, even if it was just to be part of a medical experiment. CRY-O-GENICs, Henry calls it. He says they can freeze me for a hundred years or even more, and I'll come out cool as a mint julep and just as young as I ever was. He says I seem to have done everything and everyone this little ol' century has to offer, so I may as well save myself for another time and then start all over again. They have already frozen a lot of other women—Helen of Troy, Cleopatra, Queen Guinevere, Lady Godiva, Catherine the Great, Lola Montez, and others—and Henry says they will thaw us all out when the time comes for women to rule the world. Sounds good to me. I asked him if freezing would make my waist any smaller, but he said he loved me just the way I was and he didn't know why I allowed myself to be tyrannized by societal notions of feminine beauty. Those little green men, they're so sensitive, they sure know what to say. So, Diary, don't cry for me—I'll be back.

Tomorrow is another day ....brrrrrrrh.